KEITH DOUGLAS

Keith Douglas (1920–44) ... ...
at Christ's Hospital School, continued at Oxford, and
thereafter in the army and in the Middle East. By the time he
was killed in Normandy, aged only twenty-four, in June 1944,
he had achieved a body of work that singled him out as the
most brilliant and promising English poet of the Second
World War.

Ted Hughes (1930–98) was born in Yorkshire. His first book,
The Hawk in the Rain, was published in 1957. His last
collection, *Birthday Letters*, was published in 1998 and won the
Whitbread Book of the Year, the Forward Prize and the T. S.
Eliot Prize. He was appointed Poet Laureate in 1984 and
awarded the Order of Merit in 1998.

IN THE POET-TO-POET SERIES

W. H. AUDEN – Poems selected by John Fuller
JOHN BERRYMAN – Poems selected by Michael Hofmann
JOHN BETJEMAN – Poems selected by Hugo Williams
ROBERT BROWNING – Poems selected by Douglas Dunn
ROBERT BURNS – Poems selected by Don Paterson
SAMUEL TAYLOR COLERIDGE – Poems selected by James
  Fenton
EMILY DICKINSON – Poems selected by Ted Hughes
KEITH DOUGLAS – Poems selected by Ted Hughes
JOHN DRYDEN – Poems selected by Charles Tomlinson
T. S. ELIOT – Prufrock and Other Observations
T. S. ELIOT – Four Quartets
THOMAS HARDY – Poems selected by Tom Paulin
GEORGE HERBERT – Poems selected by Jo Shapcott
HOMER – War Music, by Christopher Logue
A. E. HOUSMAN – Poems selected by Alan Hollinghurst
TED HUGHES – Poems selected by Simon Armitage
JOHN KEATS – Poems selected by Andrew Motion
ROBERT LOWELL – Poems selected by Michael Hofmann
LOUIS MACNEICE – Poems selected by Michael Longley
WILFRED OWEN – Poems selected by Jon Stallworthy
SYLVIA PLATH – Poems selected by Ted Hughes
EZRA POUND – Poems selected by Thom Gunn
WILLIAM SHAKESPEARE – Poems selected by Ted Hughes
JONATHAN SWIFT – Poems selected by Derek Mahon
ALFRED, LORD TENNYSON – Poems selected by Mick Imlah
DYLAN THOMAS – Poems selected by Derek Mahon
WILLIAM WORDSWORTH – Poems selected by Seamus
  Heaney
W. B. YEATS – Poems selected by Seamus Heaney
20TH-CENTURY SCOTTISH POEMS – Selected by Douglas
  Dunn

KEITH DOUGLAS

Poems selected by TED HUGHES

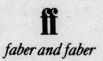

faber and faber

First published in 1964
by Faber and Faber Limited
3 Queen Square London WC1N 3AU
This edition published in 2006

Photoset by RefineCatch Ltd, Bungay, Suffolk
Printed in England by Bookmarque Ltd, Croydon

A CIP record for this book
is available from the British Library

ISBN 978–0–571–23038–9
     0–571–23038–5

10 9 8 7 6 5 4 3 2 1

Contents

Preface

Keith Castellain Douglas was born at Tunbridge Wells, Kent, on 24 January 1920. As schoolboy and student he attended Christ's Hospital and Merton College, Oxford, before enlisting in the army. In 1941 he was posted to the Middle East and served as a tank commander in the desert campaign. His prose book *Alamein to Zem Zem* gives a vivid account of the fighting. After recovering from a wound in Palestine he returned to England in 1943 to train for the European campaign. He was killed near the village of St Pierre in Normandy on 9 June 1944, three days after D-Day.

Ted Hughes, one of the poet's greatest admirers, published a selection from Douglas's poems in 1964. This can now be seen as a turning-point in Douglas's posthumous reputation. Previously he had been appreciated only by a discerning few; from now on his reputation gathered momentum. A new *Collected Poems* (for which J. C. Hall joined John Waller and G. S. Fraser as editors) appeared in 1966, followed by a fully annotated *Complete Poems* in 1978, painstakingly edited by Desmond Graham. This has been continuously in print. Side by side with the poems have been several editions of *Alamein to Zem Zem* (including one in Penguin Modern Classics) and an excellent biography by Desmond Graham, who has also edited the poet's *Letters*. These publications carry illustrations which show Douglas as also a talented artist.

A word about the texts. This selection contains only the poems chosen by Ted Hughes in 1964, for which he went to the *Collected Poems* of 1951. However, for the sake of consistency, they are here presented in the texts of *The Complete Poems*. In most cases the changes, if any, are of minor importance, but in two instances – 'Bête Noire' and 'Landscape with Figures' – the changes are quite significant, resulting in longer poems. In a third case, 'Search for a God', the single poem later became the opening section of a longer piece, 'A God is Buried'; it is printed here in its original version, which Douglas had seen fit to print, and which Hughes selected – though in a text consistent with that which appears in the *Collected Poems*. Finally, 'Forgotten the Red Leaves' is retitled 'Pleasures'.

Ted Hughes' Introduction is reprinted exactly as it appeared in 1964. He wrote about Douglas at greater length elsewhere, but scarcely more perceptively than here. For many it was their first introduction to an outstanding poet. We can only rejoice that Keith Douglas achieved so much, and so distinctively, before war silenced him at the age of twenty-four.

J. C. HALL (2005)

J. C. Hall first met Keith Douglas at Oxford and is now his literary executor.

Introduction

Keith Douglas was born in 1920 and killed in Normandy in 1944. This selection contains not quite half of his surviving poetry.

When his *Collected Poems* were first published in 1951, by Editions Poetry London Ltd, with notes and introduction, edited by John Waller and G. S. Fraser, he appeared primarily interesting, to most of his readers, as a 'war-poet', and as such seems to have been largely forgotten. Now, twenty years after his death, it is becoming clear that he offers more than just a few poems about war, and that every poem he wrote, whether about war or not, has some special value. His poetry in general seems to be of some special value. It is still very much alive, and even providing life. And the longer it lives, the fresher it looks.

The first poem printed here, 'Encounter with a God', is dated 1936. It is quite limited in scope, and comes properly into the category of juvenilia, but it accomplishes its job, not an easy one, as brilliantly and surely as anything Douglas ever did. And the qualities that create and distinguish his most important later work are already there.

It is not enough to say that the language is utterly simple, the musical inflection of it peculiarly honest and charming, the technique flawless. The language is also extremely forceful; or rather, it reposes at a point it could only have reached, this very moment, by a feat of great strength. And the inflexion of the voice has a bluntness that might be challenging if it were not so frank, and so clearly the advance of an unusually aware mind. As for the technique, insofar as it can be considered separately, there is nothing dead or asleep in it, nothing tactless, and such subtlety of movement, such economy of means, such composition of cadences, would do credit to any living poet. And behind that, ordering its directions, the essentially practical cast of his energy, his impatient, razor energy.

In his nine years of accomplished writing, Douglas

developed rapidly. Leaving his virtuoso juvenilia, his poetry passed through two roughly distinguishable phases, and began to clarify into a third. The literary influences on this progress seem to have been few. To begin with, perhaps he takes Auden's language over pretty whole, but he empties it of its intellectual concerns, turns it into the practical experience of life, and lets a few minor colours of the late 1930s poetry schools creep in. But his temperament is so utterly modern he seems to have no difficulty with the terrible, suffocating, maternal octopus of ancient English poetic tradition.

The first phase of his growth shows itself in the poem titled 'Pleasures'. He has lost nothing since 'Encounter with a God', but gained a new range of imagination, a new ease of transition from image to image. Yet in this particular poem the fairyland images are being remembered by one still partly under their spell, indulging the dream, and this mode of immaturity is the mark of this first phase, which lasts until he leaves Oxford in 1940.

Before he leaves, a poem titled 'The Deceased' heralds the next stage. Here, the picturesque or merely decorative side of his imagery disappears; his descriptive powers sharpen to realism. The impression is of a sudden mobilizing of the poet's will, a clearing of his vision, as if from sitting considering possibilities and impossibilities he had stood up to act. Pictures of things no longer interest him much: he wants their substance, their nature, and their consequences in life. At once, and quite suddenly, his mind is whole, as if united by action, and he produces poetry that is both original and adult. Already, in this poem 'The Deceased', we can see what is most important of all about Douglas. He has not simply added poems to poetry, or evolved a sophistication. He is a renovator of language. It is not that he uses words in jolting combinations, or with titanic extravagance, or curious precision. His triumph lies in the way he renews the simplicity of ordinary talk, and he does this by infusing every word with a burning exploratory freshness of mind – partly impatience, partly exhilaration at speaking the forbidden thing, partly sheer casual ease of penetration. The music that goes along with this, the unresting variety of intonation and movement within his patterns, is the natural path of such confident, candid thinking.

There is nothing studied about this new language. Its air of improvisation is a vital part of its purity. It has the trenchancy of an inspired jotting, yet leaves no doubt about the completeness and subtlety of his impressions, or the thoroughness of his artistic conscience. The poem titled 'Egypt', for instance, could be a diary note, yet how could it be improved as a poem?

The war brought his gift to maturity, or to a first maturity. In a sense, war was his ideal subject: the burning away of all human pretensions in the ray cast by death. This was the vision, the unifying generalization that shed the meaning and urgency into all his observations and particulars: not truth is beauty only, but truth kills everybody. The truth of a man is the doomed man in him or his dead body. Poem after poem circles this idea, as if his mind were tethered. At the bottom of it, perhaps, is his private muse, not a romantic symbol of danger and temptation, but the plain foreknowledge of his own rapidly-approaching end – a foreknowledge of which he becomes fully conscious in two of his finest poems. This sets his writing apart from that of Hemingway, with which it shares certain features. Hemingway tried to imagine the death that Douglas had foresuffered. Douglas had no time, and perhaps no disposition, to cultivate the fruity deciduous tree of How To Live. He showed in his poetry no concern for man in society. The murderous skeleton in the body of a girl, the dead men being eaten by dogs on the moonlit desert, the dead man behind the mirror, these items of circumstantial evidence are steadily out-arguing all his high spirits and hopefulness.

Technically, each of the poems of this second phase rests on some single objective core, a scene or event or thing. But one or two of them, and one in particular, start something different: the poems are 'On a Return from Egypt' and 'Simplify me when I'm Dead'. Their inner form is characterized not by a single object of attraction, but a constellation of statements. In the second of these poems, more liberated than the first, Douglas consummates his promise. Here he has invented a style that seems able to deal poetically with whatever it comes up against. It is not an exalted verbal activity to be attained for short periods, through abstinence, or a submerged dream treasure to be fished up when the everyday brain is half-drugged. It is a language for the whole mind, at its most wakeful, and in all situations. A utility general-purpose style, as, for instance, Shakespeare's was, that combines a colloquial prose readiness with poetic breadth, a ritual intensity and music of an exceedingly high order with clear direct feeling, and yet in the end is nothing but casual speech. This is an achievement for which we can be grateful.

TED HUGHES (1964)

KEITH DOUGLAS

Encounter with a God

Ono-no-komache the poetess
sat on the ground among her flowers,
sat in her delicate-patterned dress
thinking of the rowers,
thinking of the god Daikoku.

Thinking of the rock pool
and carp in the waterfall at night.
Daikoku in accordance with the rule
is beautiful, she said, with a slight
tendency to angles.

But Daikoku came
who had been drinking all night
with the greenish gods of chance and fame.
He was rotund standing in the moonlight,
with a round, white paunch.

Who said
I am not beautiful,
I do not wish to be wonderfully made,
I am intoxicated dutiful daughter,
and I will not be in a poem.

But the poetess sat still
holding her head and making verses:
'How intricate and peculiarly well-
arranged the symmetrical belly-purses
of lord Daikoku.'

1936

Famous Men

And now no longer sung,
not mourning, not remembered
more under the sun,

not enough their deserved
praise. The quick movement of dactyls
does not compensate them.

The air is advertised of seas
they smote, from green to copper.
These were merciful men.

And think, like plates lie deep
licked clean their skulls,
rest beautifully, staring.

1935

Pleasures

Forgotten the red leaves painting the temple in summer,
Forgotten my squirrel in his dark chamber,
The great turtle and the catamaran;
Rivers, where the mosaic stones are found.

That church, amputated by high explosive,
Where priests no more lift up their murmurous Latin,
And only the sun, a solitary worshipper,
Tiptoes towards the altar and rests there.

These and the hazy tropic where I lived
In tall seas where the bright fish go like footmen
Down the blue corridors about their business –
The jewelled skulls are down there – I have forgotten,

Almost forgot. How slowly they return
Like princes into the rooms they once owned. How dimly
I see the imaginary moon, the magic painter
Of wide, deserted acres with splendour and silence.

Once on Monte Nero in the spring
Some peasant girl fashioned for love and work
Taught me a smile that I had forgotten.
It is so hard to speak that language now.

Almost forgot, how slowly they return
Like princes into the halls they once owned.

1938

Images

The small men walk about antlike,
And the bell tolls. God created these
Beautiful or angular, not different.

The straight men are not there now
And their dark spears do not lean against the sun.
Not any more, since the bell has begun tolling.

The priests were acquainted with them,
Making chips in the pyramids,
At intervals in the warm stone.

The bell will go on tolling
To kings on their marble bases.
But these are the unacknowledged rulers.

And understanding the bell they do not hear it,
But walk over the hilltop
Into their rarer climate.

1935

Oxford

At home, as in no other city, here
summer holds her breath in a dark street
the trees nocturnally scented, lovers like moths
go by silently on the footpaths
and spirits of the young wait
cannot be expelled, multiply each year.

In the meadows, walks, over the walls
the sunlight, far-travelled, tired and content,
warms the recollections of old men, touching
the hand of the scholar on his book, marching
through quadrangles and arches, at last spent
it leans through the stained windows and falls.

This then is the city of young men, of beginning,
ideas, trials, pardonable follies,
the lightness, seriousness and sorrow of youth.
And the city of the old, looking for truth,
browsing for years, the mind's seven bellies
filled, become legendary figures, seeming

stones of the city, her venerable towers;
dignified, clothed by erudition and time.
For them it is not a city but an existence;
outside which everything is a pretence:
within, the leisurely immortals dream,
venerated and spared by the ominous hours.

Army, Oxford, 1941

Absence

The long curtained French-windows conceal
the company at dinner by candlelight.
I am the solitary person on the lawn,
dressed up silver by the moon.
The bush on my left sleeps, the tree on my right
is awake but stays motionless to feel,

as I and Cupid on his ornament stone,
how the whole evening here discourses
and the stars too lean nearer to the earth,
for their traditional splendour pours forth
much more in such unpopulous places,
almost litters the trees like rain.

So the minutes assemble at first in silence
till here or there the speech of ghosts or leaves
is audible. And it appears each grieves,
the garden with its composite voice sighing:
She is not here, and you who come instead
shew by your attitude, she's dead.

1940

A Ballet

How cleverly the choreographer
and costumier combine –
the effects fine, and the young lady's line
impeccable. With what grace her arabesque
he caps with an entrechat, this stunningly dressed
young person, her partner.

All the colours of spring
they are dressed in,
they whirl about,
and the dance over, they gracefully leap out.

But here they come again, I'm certain, or
is this not the fair
young sylph? I declare
she has a dead face and a yellow eye
and he has no limbs – how dreadfully spry
he is on his stumps:
he bleeds, but he jumps
ten feet at a prance.
I don't like this dance.

1940

The Deceased

He was a reprobate I grant
and always liquored till his money went.
His hair depended in a noose from
his pale brow. His eyes were dumb;
like prisoners in their cavernous slots, were
settled in attitudes of despair.
You who God bless you never sunk so low
censure and pray for him that he was so;
and with his failings you regret the verses
the fellow made, probably between curses,
probably in the extremes of moral decay,
but he wrote them in a sincere way:
and seems to have felt a sort of pain
to which your imagination cannot attain.

1940

Extension to Francis Thompson

Look in earth and air to catch
his mineral or electric eye.
And in the universe his voice
assumes perfect diversity.

The natural laws his angels are
and circumspectly go about
leaving marks the learned know
one for man to follow out.

Leo in drawing Deirdre's lips
drew as hand and pen were sent
by heaven. This perfection slips
through the hands to the instrument.

Expert diplomats' good taste
the curious statement of a child
or in his enamelled case
the doughty beetle hard and wild.

All in different degrees
embody the celestial thing
and the wise man will learn of these
analysis in worshipping.

   [pub. January 1941]

Search for a God

Turn away from Monte Nero, that mountain
to the west. Turn your back on the white town
of Gorizia, plastered with notices and swarming
with soldiers. Cross the green Isonzo: go down

by the ruined palace of the archbishop, the machine-gun
   schools,
and a company of the Alpini with their mules.
Now uphill to the woods where hundreds of saplings hide
where a generation of men and trees died.

And where the bright blood and shrapnel are sunk in grass
the golden oriole fluting in a cool hollow
colours the silence. These musical spirits pass
ahead and to the left. Now if you follow

you will come where high explosive could not move
the god interred beneath this flowering grove,
but he has slept two hundred decades here.

No music will wake his marble: not yet,
still he must lie in soil and forget
another madness begun this year.

Canoe

Well, I am thinking this may be my last
summer, but cannot lose even a part of
pleasure in the old-fashioned art of
idleness. I cannot stand aghast

at whatever doom hovers in the background;
while grass and buildings and the somnolent river,
who know they are allowed to last for ever,
exchange between them the whole subdued sound

of this hot time. What sudden fearful fate
can deter my shade wandering next year
from a return? Whistle and I will hear
and come another evening, when this boat

travels with you alone towards Iffley:
as you lie looking up for thunder again,
this cool touch does not betoken rain;
it is my spirit that kisses your mouth lightly.

[pub. May 1940]

Soissons

M. l'Épicier in his white hat
in an outhouse by the cathedral, makes
devils from the selfsame stone
men used in the religious century.
The cathedral itself in new masonry
of white, stands openly in this sunlit town,
Soissons. Down the long hill snakes
the hard hot road into the town's heart.

In the evening when the late sunlight abandons
buildings still glimmering from shadow on shadow
someone leans from a window eavesdropping our
strange voices so late in the cathedral square.
From the barracks of the 19th Regiment you can hear
the equivalent of Lights Out. Now the sweet-sour
wine clambers in our heads. Go in. Tomorrow
tiptoes with us along the dark landing.

'A Laon, belle cathédrale', making
a wave of his white hat, explains
the maker of gargoyles. So we take
a route for Laon and Rheims leaving you
Soissons, a simplified medieval view
taken from a Book of Hours. How dark
seems the whole country we enter. Now it rains,
the trees like ominous old men are shaking.

1940

Stars

(For Antoinette)

The stars still marching in extended order
move out of nowhere into nowhere. Look, they are halted
on a vast field tonight, true no man's land.
Far down the sky with sword and belt must stand
Orion. For commissariat of this exalted
war-company, the Wain. No fabulous border

could swallow all this bravery, no band
will ever face them: nothing but discipline
has mobilized and still maintains them. So
Time and his ancestors have seen them. So
always to fight disorder is their business,
and victory continues in their hand.

From under the old hills to overhead,
and down there marching on the hills again
their camp extends. There go the messengers,
Comets, with greetings of ethereal officers
from tent to tent. Yes, we look up with pain
at distant comrades and plains we cannot tread.

[1939]

John Anderson

John Anderson, a scholarly gentleman
advancing with his company in the attack
received some bullets through him as he ran.

So his creative brain whirled, and he fell back
in the bloody dust, (it was a fine day there
and warm). Blood turned his tunic black

while past his desperate final stare
the other simple soldiers run
and leave the hero unaware.

Apt epitaph or pun
he could not hit upon, to grace
a scholar's death; he only eyed the sun.

But I think, the last moment of his gaze
beheld the father of gods and men,
Zeus, leaning from heaven as he dies,

whom in his swoon he hears again
summon Apollo in the Homeric tongue:
Descend Phoebus and cleanse the stain

of dark blood from the body of John Anderson.
Give him to Death and Sleep,
who'll bear him as they can

out of the range of darts, to the broad vale
of Lycia; there lay him in a deep
solemn content on some bright dale.

And the brothers, Sleep and Death
lift up John Anderson at his last breath.

1940

The Marvel

A baron of the sea, the great tropic
swordfish, spreadeagled on the thirsty deck
where sailors killed him, in the bright Pacific

yielded to the sharp enquiring blade
the eye which guided him and found his prey
in the dim country where he was a lord;

which is an instrument forged in semi-darkness
yet taken from the corpse of this strong traveller
becomes a powerful enlarging glass

reflecting the unusual sun's heat.
With it a sailor writes on the hot wood
the name of a harlot in his last port.

For it is one most curious device
of many, kept by the interesting waves –
and I suppose the querulous soft voice

of mariners who rotted into ghosts
digested by the gluttonous tides
could recount many. Let them be your hosts

and take you where their forgotten ships lie
with fishes going over the tall masts –
all this emerges from the burning eye.

And to engrave that word the sun goes through
with the power of the sea,
writing her name and a marvel too.

Linney Head, Wales, [May] 1941

Time Eating

Ravenous Time has flowers for his food
at Autumn – yet can cleverly make good
each petal: devours animals and men,
but for ten dead he can create ten.

If you enquire how secretly you've come
to mansize from the bigness of a stone
it will appear it's his art made you rise
so gradually to your proper size.

But while he makes he eats: the very part
where he began, even the elusive heart
Time's ruminative tongue will wash
and slow juice masticate all flesh.

That volatile huge intestine holds
material and abstract in its folds:
thought and ambition melt, and even the world
will alter, in that catholic belly curled.

But Time, who ate my love, you cannot make
such another. You who can remake
the lizard's tail and the bright snakeskin
cannot, cannot. That you gobbled in
too quick: and though you brought me from a boy
you can make no more of me, only destroy.

Wickwar, Glos., 1941

The Prisoner

Today, Cheng, I touched your face
with two fingers, as a gesture of love,
for I can never prove enough
by sight or sense your strange grace;

but like moths my hands return
to your skin, that's luminous
like a lamp in a paper house,
and touch, to teach love and learn.

I think a thousand hours are gone
that so, like gods, we'd occupy:
but alas, Cheng, I cannot tell why,
today I touched a mask stretched on the stone-

hard face of death. There was the urge
to escape the bright flesh and emerge
of the ambitious cruel bone.

Royal Military College, Sandhurst, 1940

Song

Dotards do not think
but slowly slowly turn
eyes that have seen too much
expecting the soft touch
of Fate who cannot burn
but is a last drink,
a night drink, an opiate,
and almost comes too late.

I who could feel pain
a month, a month ago
and pleasure for my mind
and other pleasure find
like any dotard now
am wearily sat down,
a dull man, a prisoner
in a dull chamber.

You who richly live
look at me, look at me;
stirred to talk with you
I speak a word or two
like an effigy.
What answer will you give?
Can you wake the drugged man?
I wonder if you can.

Wickwar, Glos., 1941

Simplify me when I'm Dead

Remember me when I am dead
and simplify me when I'm dead.

As the processes of earth
strip off the colour and the skin
take the brown hair and blue eye

and leave me simpler than at birth
when hairless I came howling in
as the moon came in the cold sky.

Of my skeleton perhaps
so stripped, a learned man will say
'He was of such a type and intelligence,' no more.

Thus when in a year collapse
particular memories, you may
deduce, from the long pain I bore

the opinions I held, who was my foe
and what I left, even my appearance
but incidents will be no guide.

Time's wrong-way telescope will show
a minute man ten years hence
and by distance simplified.

Through that lens see if I seem
substance or nothing: of the world
deserving mention or charitable oblivion

not by momentary spleen
or love into decision hurled
leisurely arrive at an opinion.

Remember me when I am dead
and simplify me when I'm dead.

[? May 1941]

The Sea Bird

Walking along beside the beach
where the Mediterranean turns in sleep
under the cliffs' demiarch

through a curtain of thought I see
a dead bird and a live bird
the dead eyeless, but with a bright eye

the live bird discovered me
and stepped from a black rock into the air —
I turn from the dead bird to watch him fly,

electric, brilliant blue,
beneath he is orange, like flame,
colours I can't believe are so,

as legendary flowers bloom
incendiary in tint, so swift he
searches about the sky for room,

towering like the cliffs of this coast
with his stiletto wing
and orange on his breast:

he has consumed and drained
the colours of the sea
and the yellow of this tidal ground

till he escapes the eye, or is a ghost
and in a moment has come down
crept into the dead bird, ceased to exist.

[pub. January 1943]

The Hand

The hand is perfect in itself – the five
fingers though changing attitude depend
on a golden point, the imaginary true focal
to which infinities of motion and shape are yoked.
There is no beginning to the hand, no end,
and the bone retains its proportion in the grave.

I can transmute this hand, changing each
finger to a man or a woman, and the hills
behind, drawn in their relation:
and to more than men, women, hills, by alteration
of symbols standing for the fingers, for the whole hand,
this alchemy is not difficult to teach,

this making a set of pictures; this drawing
shapes within the shapes of the hand –
an ordinary translation of forms. But hence,
try to impose arguments
whose phrases, each upon a digit, tend
to the centre of reasoning, the mainspring.

To do this is drilling the mind, still a recruit,
for the active expeditions of his duty
when he must navigate alone the wild
cosmos, as the Jew wanders the world:
and we, watching the tracks of him at liberty
like the geometry of feet
upon a shore, constructed in the sand,
look for the proportions, the form of an immense hand.

Nathanya, Palestine,[October] 1941

Syria

These grasses, ancient enemies
waiting at the edge of towns
conceal a movement of live stones,
the lizards with hooded eyes
of hostile miraculous age.

It is not snow on the green space
of hilltops, only towns of white
whose trees are populous with fruit
and girls whose velvet beauty is
handed down to them, gentle ornaments.

Here I am a stranger clothed
in the separative glass cloak
of strangeness. The dark eyes, the bright-mouthed
smiles, glance on the glass and break
falling like fine strange insects.

But from the grass, the inexorable lizard,
the dart of hatred for all strangers finds
in this armour, proof only against friends,
breach after breach, and like the gnat is busy
wounding the skin, leaving poison there.

[? November 1941–June 1942]

Negative Information

As lines, the unrelated symbols of
nothing you know, discovered in the clouds
idly made on paper, or by the feet of crowds
on sand, keep whatever meaning they have

and you believe they write, for some
intelligence, messages of a sort;
these curious indentations on my thought
with every week, almost with each hour come.

Perhaps you remember the fantastic moon
in the Atlantic – we descried the prisoner laden
with the thornbush and lantern –
the phosphorescence, the ship singing a sea-tune.

How we lost our circumstances that night
and, like spirits attendant on the ship
now at the mast, now on the waves, might almost dip
and soar as lightly as our entranced sight.

Against that, the girls who met us at one place
were not whores, but women old and young at once
whom accidents turned to pretty stones,
to images alight with deceptive grace.

And in general, the account of many deaths –
whose portents, which should have undone the sky,
had never come – is now received casually.
You and I are careless of these millions of wraiths.

For as often as not we meet
in dreams our own dishevelled ghosts;
and opposite, the modest hosts
of our ambition stare them out.

To this, there's no sum I can find –
the hungry omens of calamity
mixed with good signs, and all received with levity,
or indifference, by the amazed mind.

Palestine, 16 October 1941

Egypt

Aniseed has a sinful taste:
at your elbow a woman's voice
like I imagine the voice of ghosts,
demanding food. She has no grace

but, diseased and blind of an eye
and heavy with habitual dolour
listlessly finds you and I
and the table, are the same colour.

The music, the harsh talk, the fine
clash of the drinkseller's tray
are the same to her as her own whine,
she knows no variety.

And in fifteen years of living
found nothing different from death
but the difference of moving
and the nuisance of breath.

A disguise of ordure can't hide
her beauty, succumbing in a cloud
of disease, disease, apathy. My God,
the king of this country must be proud.

[Egypt, ? September 1942]

27

Behaviour of Fish in an Egyptian Tea Garden

As a white stone draws down the fish
she on the seafloor of the afternoon
draws down men's glances and their cruel wish
for love. Slyly her red lip on the spoon

slips in a morsel of ice-cream; her hands
white as a milky stone, white submarine
fronds, sink with spread fingers, lean
along the table, carmined at the ends.

A cotton magnate, an important fish
with great eyepouches and a golden mouth
through the frail reefs of furniture swims out
and idling, suspended, stays to watch.

A crustacean old man clamped to his chair
sits coldly near her and might see
her charms through fissures where the eyes should be
or else his teeth are parted in a stare.

Captain on leave, a lean dark mackerel
lies in the offing, turns himself and looks
through currents of sound. The flat-eyed flatfish sucks
on a straw, staring from its repose, laxly.

And gallants in shoals swim up and lag,
circling and passing near the white attraction;
sometimes pausing, opening a conversation:
fish pause so to nibble or tug.

Now the ice-cream is finished, is
paid for. The fish swim off on business:
and she sits alone at the table, a white stone
useless except to a collector, a rich man.

Cairo [? October] 1943

Christodoulos

Christodoulos moves, and shakes
his seven chins. He is that freak
a successful alchemist, and makes
God knows how much a week.

Out of Christodoulos' attic,
full of smoke and smells, emerge
soldiers like ants; with ants' erratic
gestures seek the pavement's verge;

weak as wounded, leaning in a knot
shout in the streets for an enemy –
the dross of Christodoulos' pot
or wastage from his alchemy.

They flow elsewhere; by swarthy portals
entering the crucibles of others
and the lesser sages' mortars:
but Christodoulos is the father

of all, he's the original wise one
from whose experiments they told
how War can be the famous stone
for turning rubbish into gold.

[Egypt, ? September 1942]

Words

Words are my instruments but not my servants;
by the white pillar of a prince I lie in wait
for them. In what the hour or the minute invents,
in a web formally meshed or inchoate,
these fritillaries are come upon, trapped:
hot-coloured, or the cold scarabs a thousand years
old, found in cerements and unwrapped.
The catch and the ways of catching are diverse.
For instance this stooping man, the bones of whose face are
like the hollow birds' bones, is a trap for words.
And the pockmarked house bleached by the glare
whose insides war has dried out like gourds
attracts words. There are those who capture them
in hundreds, keep them prisoners in black
bottles, release them at exercise and clap them back.
But I keep words only a breath of time
turning in the lightest of cages – uncover
and let them go: sometimes they escape for ever.

El Ballah [General Hospital] 1943

Bête Noire [fragments]

A (I)

Yes, I too have a particular monster
a toad or worm curled in the belly
stirring, eating at times I cannot foretell, he
is the thing I can admit only once to
anyone, never to those who have not their own.
Never to those who are happy, whose easy language
I speak well, though with a stranger's accent.

A (II)

This is my particular monster. I know him;
he walks about inside me: I'm his house
and his landlord. He's my evacuee
taking a respite from hell in me
he decorates his room of course
to remind him of home. He often talks of going –

such a persuasive gentleman he is
I believe him, I go out quite sure
that I'll come back and find him gone
but does he go? Not him. No, he's a one
who likes his joke, he won't sit waiting for
me to come home, but comes

B

The Beast is a jailer
allows me out on parole
brings me back by telepathy
is inside my mind
breaks into my conversation with his own words,
speaking out of my mouth
can overthrow me in a moment
writes what I write, or edits it (censors it)
takes a dislike to my friends and sets me against them
can take away pleasure
is absent for long periods, is never expected when he
    returns
has several forms and disguises
makes enemies for me
can be overthrown by me, if I have help.
I have been trying to get help for about eleven years.
Three times I got help.
If this is a game, it's past half time and the beast is
    winning.

C

The trumpet man to take it away
blows a hot break in a beautiful way
ought to snap my fingers and tap my toes
but I sit at my table and nobody knows
I've got a beast on my back.

A medieval animal with a dog's face
Notre Dame or Chartres is his proper place
but here he is in the Piccadilly
sneering at the hot musicians' skill. He
is the beast on my back.

Suppose we dance, suppose we run away
into the street, or the underground
he'd come with us. It's his day.
Don't kiss me. Don't put your arm round
and touch the beast on my back

D

If at times my eyes are lenses
through which the brain explores
constellations of feeling
my ears yielding like swinging doors
admit princes to the corridors
into the mind, do not envy me.
I have a beast on my back

[February–March 1944]

Dead Men

Tonight the moon inveigles them
to love: they infer from her gaze
her tacit encouragement.
Tonight the white dresses and the jasmin scent
in the streets. I in another place
see the white dresses glimmer like moths. Come

to the west, out of that trance, my heart –
here the same hours have illumined
sleepers who are condemned or reprieved
and those whom their ambitions have deceived;
the dead men, whom the wind
powders till they are like dolls: they tonight

rest in the sanitary earth perhaps
or where they died, no one has found them
or in their shallow graves the wild dog
discovered and exhumed a face or a leg
for food: the human virtue round them
is a vapour tasteless to a dog's chops.

All that is good of them, the dog consumes.
You would not know, now the mind's flame is gone,
more than the dog knows: you would forget
but that you see your own mind burning yet
and till you stifle in the ground will go on
burning the economical coal of your dreams.

Then leave the dead in the earth, an organism
not capable of resurrection, like mines,
less durable than the metal of a gun,
a casual meal for a dog, nothing but the bone
so soon. But tonight no lovers see the lines
of the moon's face as the lines of cynicism.

And the wise man is the lover
who in his planetary love revolves
without the traction of reason or time's control
and the wild dog finding meat in a hole
is a philosopher. The prudent mind resolves
on the lover's or the dog's attitude for ever.

[pub. March 1943]

Mersa

This blue halfcircle of sea
moving transparently
on sand as pale as salt
was Cleopatra's hotel:

here is a guesthouse built
and broken utterly, since.
An amorous modern prince
lived in this scoured shell.

Now from the skeletal town
the cherry skinned soldiers stroll down
to undress to idle on the white beach.
Up there, the immensely long road goes by

to Tripoli: the wind and dust reach
the secrets of the whole
poor town whose masks would still
deceive a passer-by;

faces with sightless doors
for eyes, with cracks like tears
oozing at corners. A dead tank alone
leans where the gossips stood.

I see my feet like stones
underwater. The logical little fish
converge and nip the flesh
imagining I am one of the dead.

[after October 1942]

Cairo Jag

Shall I get drunk or cut myself a piece of cake,
a pasty Syrian with a few words of English
or the Turk who says she is a princess – she dances
apparently by levitation? Or Marcelle, Parisienne
always preoccupied with her dull dead lover:
she has all the photographs and his letters
tied in a bundle and stamped *Décedé* in mauve ink.
All this takes place in a stink of jasmin.

But there are the streets dedicated to sleep
stenches and the sour smells, the sour cries
do not disturb their application to slumber
all day, scattered on the pavement like rags
afflicted with fatalism and hashish. The women
offering their children brown-paper breasts
dry and twisted, elongated like the skull,
Holbein's signature. But this stained white town
is something in accordance with mundane conventions –
Marcelle drops her Gallic airs and tragedy
suddenly shrieks in Arabic about the fare
with the cabman, links herself so
with the somnambulists and legless beggars:
it is all one, all as you have heard.

But by a day's travelling you reach a new world
the vegetation is of iron
dead tanks, gun barrels split like celery
the metal brambles have no flowers or berries
and there are all sorts of manure, you can imagine
the dead themselves, their boots, clothes and possessions
clinging to the ground, a man with no head
has a packet of chocolate and a souvenir of Tripoli.

[El Ballah, General Hospital, ? February 1943]

To Kristin Yingcheng Olga Milena

Women of four countries
the four phials full of essences
of green England, legendary China,
cold Europe, Arabic Spain, a finer
four poisons for the subtle senses
than any in medieval inventories.

Here I give back perforce
the sweet wine to the grape
give the dark plant its juices
what every creature uses
by natural law will seep
back to the natural source.

[? March 1944]

How to Kill

Under the parabola of a ball,
a child turning into a man,
I looked into the air too long.
The ball fell in my hand, it sang
in the closed fist: *Open Open*
Behold a gift designed to kill.

Now in my dial of glass appears
the soldier who is going to die.
He smiles, and moves about in ways
his mother knows, habits of his.
The wires touch his face: I cry
NOW. Death, like a familiar, hears

and look, has made a man of dust
of a man of flesh. This sorcery
I do. Being damned, I am amused
to see the centre of love diffused
and the waves of love travel into vacancy.
How easy it is to make a ghost.

The weightless mosquito touches
her tiny shadow on the stone,
and with how like, how infinite
a lightness, man and shadow meet.
They fuse. A shadow is a man
when the mosquito death approaches.

[? Tunisia–Cairo, 1943]

Landscape With Figures

I

Perched on a great fall of air
a pilot or angel looking down
on some eccentric chart, the plain
dotted with the useless furniture
discerns crouching on the sand vehicles
squashed dead or still entire, stunned
like beetles: scattered wingcases and
legs, heads, show when the haze settles.
But you who like Thomas come
to poke fingers in the wounds
find monuments, and metal posies:
on each disordered tomb
the steel is torn into fronds
by the lunatic explosive.

[? Tel Aviv, April 1943]

II

On scrub and sand the dead men wriggle
in their dowdy clothes. They are mimes
who express silence and futile aims
enacting this prone and motionless struggle
at a queer angle to the scenery
crawling on the boards of the stage like walls
deaf to the one who opens his mouth and calls
silently. The décor is terrible tracery
of iron. The eye and mouth of each figure
bear the cosmetic blood and hectic
colours death has the only list of.
A yard more, and my little finger

could trace the maquillage of these stony actors
I am the figure writhing on the backcloth.

[? Tel Aviv, April 1943]

III

I am the figure burning in hell
and the figure of the grave priest
observing everyone who passed
and that of the lover. I am all
the aimless pilgrims, the pedants and courtiers
more easily you believe me a pioneer
and a murdering villain without fear
without remorse hacking at the throat. Yes
I am all these and I am the craven
the remorseful the distressed
penitent: not passing from life to life
but all these angels and devils are driven
into my mind like beasts. I am possessed,
the house whose wall contains the dark strife
the arguments of hell with heaven.

[? April–September 1943]

Aristocrats

The noble horse with courage in his eye,
clean in the bone, looks up at a shellburst:
away fly the images of the shires
but he puts the pipe back in his mouth.

Peter was unfortunately killed by an 88;
it took his leg away, he died in the ambulance.
I saw him crawling on the sand, he said
It's most unfair, they've shot my foot off.

How can I live among this gentle
obsolescent breed of heroes, and not weep?
Unicorns, almost,
for they are fading into two legends
in which their stupidity and chivalry
are celebrated. Each, fool and hero, will be an immortal.

These plains were their cricket pitch
and in the mountains the tremendous drop fences
brought down some of the runners. Here then
under the stones and earth they dispose themselves,
I think with their famous unconcern.
It is not gunfire I hear, but a hunting horn.

Tunisia 1943

I Listen to the Desert Wind

I listen to the desert wind
that will not blow her from my mind;
the stars will not put down a hand,
the moon's ignorant of my wound

moving negligently across
by clouds and cruel tracts of space
as in my brain by nights and days
moves the reflection of her face.

Like a bird my sleepless eye
skims the sands who now deny
the violent heat they have by day
as she denies her former way

all the elements agree
with her, to have no sympathy
for my impertinent misery
as wonderful and hard as she.

O turn in the dark bed again
and give to him what once was mine
and I'll turn as you turn
and kiss my swarthy mistress pain.

Wadi Natrun, [October] 1942

Vergissmeinnicht

Three weeks gone and the combatants gone
returning over the nightmare ground
we found the place again, and found
the soldier sprawling in the sun.

The frowning barrel of his gun
overshadowing. As we came on
that day, he hit my tank with one
like the entry of a demon.

Look. Here in the gunpit spoil
the dishonoured picture of his girl
who has put: *Steffi. Vergissmeinnicht*
in a copybook gothic script.

We see him almost with content,
abased, and seeming to have paid
and mocked at by his own equipment
that's hard and good when he's decayed.

But she would weep to see today
how on his skin the swart flies move;
the dust upon the paper eye
and the burst stomach like a cave.

For here the lover and killer are mingled
who had one body and one heart.
And death who had the soldier singled
has done the lover mortal hurt.

   Tunisia [May–June] 1943

Gallantry

The Colonel in a casual voice
spoke into the microphone a joke
which through a hundred earphones broke
into the ears of a doomed race.

Into the ears of the doomed boy, the fool
whose perfectly mannered flesh fell
in opening the door for a shell
as he had learnt to do at school.

Conrad luckily survived the winter:
he wrote a letter to welcome
the auspicious spring: only his silken
intentions severed with a single splinter.

Was George fond of little boys?
We always suspected it,
but who will say: since George was hit
we never mention our surmise.

It was a brave thing the Colonel said,
but the whole sky turned too hot
and the three heroes never heard what
it was, gone deaf with steel and lead.

But the bullets cried with laughter,
the shells were overcome with mirth,
plunging their heads in steel and earth –
(the air commented in a whisper).

El Ballah, General Hospital, 1943

Snakeskin and Stone

I praise a snakeskin or a stone:
a bald head and a public speech
I hate: the serpent's lozenges
are calligraphy, and it is
the truth these cryptograms teach
the pebble is truth alone.

Complication is belonging to the snake
who is as subtle as his gold, black, green
and it is right the stone is old
and smooth, utterly cruel and old.
These two are two pillars. Between
stand all the buildings truth can make,

a whole city, inhabited by lovers
murderers, workmen and artists
not much recognized: all
who have no memorial
but are mere men. Even the lowest
never made himself a mask of words or figures.

The bald head is a desert
between country of life and country of death
between the desolate projecting ears
move the wicked explorers, the flies
who know the dead bone is beneath
and from the skin the life half out.

The words are dying in heaps
in the papers they lie in rows
awaiting burial. The speaker's mouth
like a cold sea that sucks and spews them out
with insult to their bodies. Tangled they cruise
like mariners' bodies in the grave of ships.

Borrow hair for the bald crown
borrow applause for the dead words
for you who think the desert hidden
or the words, like the dry bones, living
are fit to profit from the world.
God help the lover of snakeskin and stone.

[? El Ballah, General Hospital, 1943]

Desert Flowers

Living in a wide landscape are the flowers –
Rosenberg I only repeat what you were saying –
the shell and the hawk every hour
are slaying men and jerboas, slaying

the mind: but the body can fill
the hungry flowers and the dogs who cry words
at nights, the most hostile things of all.
But that is not new. Each time the night discards

draperies on the eyes and leaves the mind awake
I look each side of the door of sleep
for the little coin it will take
to buy the secret I shall not keep.

I see men as trees suffering
or confound the detail and the horizon.
Lay the coin on my tongue and I will sing
of what the others never set eyes on.

[? El Ballah, General Hospital, 1943]

On a Return from Egypt

To stand here in the wings of Europe
disheartened, I have come away
from the sick land where in the sun lay
the gentle sloe-eyed murderers
of themselves, exquisites under a curse;
here to exercise my depleted fury.

For the heart is a coal, growing colder
when jewelled cerulean seas change
into grey rocks, grey water-fringe,
sea and sky altering like a cloth
till colour and sheen are gone both:
cold is an opiate of the soldier.

And all my endeavours are unlucky explorers
come back, abandoning the expedition;
the specimens, the lilies of ambition
still spring in their climate, still unpicked:
but time, time is all I lacked
to find them, as the great collectors before me.

The next month, then, is a window
and with a crash I'll split the glass.
Behind it stands one I must kiss,
person of love or death
a person or a wraith,
I fear what I shall find.

[? March–April 1944]